KNOW YOUR FOOD

SUGAR AND SWEETENERS

KNOW YOUR FOOD

KNOW YOUR FOOD

Sugar and Sweeteners

JOHN PERRITANO

MASON CREST

Mason Crest
450 Parkway Drive, Suite D
Broomall, PA 19008
www.masoncrest.com

MTM Publishing, Inc.
435 West 23rd Street, #8C
New York, NY 10011
www.mtmpublishing.com

President: Valerie Tomaselli
Vice President, Book Development: Hilary Poole
Designer: Annemarie Redmond
Copyeditor: Peter Jaskowiak
Editorial Assistant: Leigh Eron

Series ISBN: 978-1-4222-3733-5
Hardback ISBN: 978-1-4222-3744-1
E-Book ISBN: 978-1-4222-8051-5

Library of Congress Cataloging-in-Publication Data
Names: Perritano, John, author.
Title: Sugar and sweeteners / by John Perritano.
Description: Broomall, PA: Mason Crest, [2018] | Series: Know your food | Audience: Ages 12+. | Audience: Grades 7 to 8. | Includes bibliographical references and index.
Identifiers: LCCN 2016053114 (print) | LCCN 2016055592 (ebook) | ISBN 9781422237441 (hardback: alk. paper) | ISBN 9781422280515 (ebook)
Subjects: LCSH: Sugars in human nutrition—Juvenile literature. | Sugars—Juvenile literature. | Sweeteners—Juvenile literature. | Food additives—Juvenile literature. | Nutrition—Juvenile literature.
Classification: LCC TX553.S8 P47 2018 (print) | LCC TX553.S8 (ebook) | DDC 641.3/08—dc23
LC record available at https://lccn.loc.gov/2016053114

Printed and bound in the United States of America.

First printing
9 8 7 6 5 4 3 2 1

TABLE OF CONTENTS

Key Icons to Look for:

Words to Understand: These words with their easy-to-understand definitions will increase the reader's understanding of the text, while building vocabulary skills.

Sidebars: This boxed material within the main text allows readers to build knowledge, gain insights, explore possibilities, and broaden their perspectives by weaving together additional information to provide realistic and holistic perspectives.

Educational Videos: Readers can view videos by scanning our QR codes, which will provide them with additional educational content to supplement the text. Examples include news coverage, moments in history, speeches, iconic sports moments, and much more.

Text-Dependent Questions: These questions send the reader back to the text for more careful attention to the evidence presented there.

Research Projects: Readers are pointed toward areas of further inquiry connected to each chapter. Suggestions are provided for projects that encourage deeper research and analysis.

Series Glossary of Key Terms: This back-of-the-book glossary contains terminology used throughout the series. Words found here increase the reader's ability to read and comprehend higher-level books and articles in this field.

SERIES INTRODUCTION

In the early 19th century, a book was published in France called *Physiologie du goût* (*The Physiology of Taste*), and since that time, it has never gone out of print. Its author was Jean Anthelme Brillat-Savarin. Brillat-Savarin is still considered to be one of the great food writers, and he was, to use our current lingo, arguably the first "foodie." Among other pearls, *Physiologie du goût* gave us one of the quintessential aphorisms about dining: "Tell me what you eat, and I will tell you what you are."

This concept was introduced to Americans in the 20th century by a nutritionist named Victor Lindlahr, who wrote simply, "You are what you eat." Lindlahr interpreted the saying literally: if you eat healthy food, he argued, you will become a healthy person.

But Brillat-Savarin likely had something a bit more metaphorical in mind. His work suggested that the dishes we create and consume have not only nutritional implications, but ethical, philosophical, and even political implications, too.

To be clear, Brillat-Savarin had a great deal to say on the importance of nutrition. In his writings he advised people to limit their intake of "floury and starchy substances," and for that reason he is sometimes considered to be the inventor of the low-carb diet. But Brillat-Savarin also took the idea of dining extremely seriously. He was devoted to the notion of pleasure in eating and was a fierce advocate of the importance of being a good host. In fact, he went so far as to say that anyone who doesn't make an effort to feed his guests "does not deserve to have friends." Brillat-Savarin also understood that food was at once deeply personal and extremely social. "Cooking is one of the oldest arts," he wrote, "and one that has rendered us the most important service in civic life."

Modern diners and cooks still grapple with the many implications of Brillat-Savarin's most famous statement. Certainly on a nutritional level, we understand that a diet that's low in fat and high in whole grains is a key to healthy living. This is no minor issue. Unless our current course is reversed, today's "obesity epidemic" is poised to significantly reduce the life spans of future generations.

Meanwhile, we are becoming increasingly aware of how the decisions we make at supermarkets can ripple outward, impacting our neighborhoods, nations, and the earth as a whole. Increasing numbers of us are demanding organically produced foods and ethically sourced ingredients. Some shoppers reject products that contain artificial ingredients like trans fats or high-fructose corn syrup. Some adopt gluten-free or vegan diets, while others "go Paleo" in the hopes of returning to a more "natural" way of eating. A simple trip to the supermarket can begin to feel like a personality test—the implicit question is not only "what does a *healthy* person eat?," but also "what does a *good* person eat?"

The Know Your Food series introduces students to these complex issues by looking at the various components that make up our meals: carbohydrates, fats, proteins, vitamins, and so on. Each volume focuses on one component and explains its function in our bodies, how it gets into food, how it changes when cooked, and what happens when we consume too much or too little. The volumes also look at food production—for example, how did the food dye called Red No. 2 end up in our food, and why was it taken out? What are genetically modified organisms, and are they safe or not? Along the way, the volumes also explore different diets, such as low-carb, low-fat, vegetarian, and gluten-free, going beyond the hype to examine their potential benefits and possible downsides.

Each chapter features definitions of key terms for that specific section, while a Series Glossary at the back provides an overview of words that are most important to the set overall. Chapters have Text-Dependent Questions at the end, to help students assess their comprehension of the most important material, as well as suggested Research Projects that will help them continue their exploration. Last but not least, QR codes accompany each chapter; students with cell phones or tablets can scan these codes for videos that will help bring the topics to life. (Those without devices can access the videos via an Internet browser; the addresses are included at the end of the Further Reading list.)

In the spirit of Brillat-Savarin, the volumes in this set look beyond nutrition to also consider various historical, political, and ethical aspects of food. Whether it's the key role that sugar played in the slave trade, the implications of industrial meat production in the fight against climate change, or the short-sighted political decisions that resulted in the water catastrophe in Flint, Michigan, the Know Your Food series introduces students to the ways in which a meal can be, in a real sense, much more than just a meal.

WHAT ARE SUGAR AND SWEETENERS?

 ## WORDS TO UNDERSTAND

calories: units of energy.

carbohydrates: chemical compounds that contain hydrogen, carbon, and oxygen atoms.

chlorophyll: the green pigment in plants that captures the energy from the sun required for photosynthesis.

diabetes: a group of blood diseases that affects the way the body processes sugars.

quantify: to numerically determine the extent of something.

synthetic: human-made.

More than 200 years ago in Philadelphia, the nation's revolutionary founders signed the Declaration of Independence and forged a constitution that secured for all Americans the "Blessings of Liberty." But Vicki Landers wasn't having any of it during the summer of 2016. The city's leaders wanted to tax her sugary soft drink. In her mind, and in the minds of others, the tax was akin to the British taxing tea, molasses, and other products during the run-up to the American Revolution (1775–1783). "It's a horrible idea," Landers railed to a newspaper reporter. "They're taking away people's rights to be able to have the things they want."

Some lawmakers hope that increasing the cost of sugary soft drinks will have public health benefits later on.

Lawmakers defended the tax as a public health measure, but Landers and others complained that sugar is not dangerous in the same way as other "bad" products that are taxed, like tobacco and alcohol. On the contrary, sugar is sweet, tasty, and, in the right amount, it is even necessary for human life. But despite the protestations, bickering, and political jockeying, Philadelphia's lawmakers passed a 1.5 cent per ounce tax on all sugary drinks sold in the city, effectively raising the price of a 20-ounce drink by 30 cents. Health experts hoped that the increased cost would decrease the consumption of sugary beverages. It's a tactic that has been effective in other situations, such as convincing people to quit smoking.

"If we go five years ahead and look back, I think this is going to be a watershed moment," Jim Krieger, executive director at Healthy Food America, told *The New York Times*, adding, "It is a good thing to drink less sugar-sweetened beverages."

How Sweet It Is

If you enjoy eating cupcakes, cookies, breakfast cereal, candy, barbeque sauce, lemonade, bottled iced tea, cakes, pies, wheat bread, bologna sandwiches, and dozens of other foods, then you like sugar. We put it in coffee and sprinkle it on our corn flakes. But most of the sugar we consume, we can't see—it comes to us as an ingredient in products such as processed foods and baked goods. Sugar not only makes food taste sweet, but it also enhances its aroma and texture. Sugar helps to turn the crust of food brown as it cooks. It also helps food retain moisture.

Americans love sugar so much that, whether we know it or not, an average adult eats 22 teaspoons of sugar per day, and the average kid eats 33 teaspoons! That's way too much, experts say. Every teaspoon of processed sugar (more on that later) contains about 130 calories and has zero nutritional value.

Yet not all sugar is bad for you. Without it, your body would have a hard time doing its job. That's because sugar is a simple carbohydrate, a substance the body uses as a source of energy. You can find simple sugars, also known as monosaccharides, in processed or refined sugar. Table sugar is an example of

THE MANY TYPES OF SUGAR

Sugar by any other name is still sugar, but it comes in many forms, including:

- **Sucrose**, or ordinary sugar. Sucrose contains fructose and dextrose.
- **Dextrose,** also known as glucose, is found in starchy foods. Your body quickly absorbs dextrose.
- **Fructose**, the natural sugar found in fruits and berries.
- **Lactose**, the sugar found in milk.
- **Maltose**, which is malt sugar.

processed sugar, also known as sucrose. Sucrose comes from processing sugarcane and sugar beets. Every time you eat a piece of cake, crack open a can of cola, or chew on a wad of bubble gum, you are consuming sucrose.

Simple sugars are also found in milk and fruit. You might have heard of someone avoiding dairy products because he or she is "lactose intolerant"; lactose is actually a form of sugar. Meanwhile, fructose is fruit sugar. Honey, maple syrup, apples, grapes, and melons are good sources of fructose. Plants produce sugar through photosynthesis, the process by which they and other organisms turn carbon dioxide and water into carbohydrates using light from the sun and chlorophyll.

ALTERNATIVE SWEETENERS

While sugar in the right amounts is necessary for life, consuming too much of it can cause a variety of health problems, ranging from diabetes to obesity (see chapter three). That is why science—and nature to some extent—has come up with alternative sweeteners, including saccharine, acesulfame potassium, cyclamate, among others.

DEATH BY SWEETNESS

In 2015, researchers at Tufts University in Boston estimated that consuming sugary drinks led to an estimated 184,000 adult deaths each year. It was the first time scientists investigated and quantified the global impact of sugar-sweetened beverages. The scientists said consuming sugary drinks, including soda, fruit drinks, energy drinks, sports drinks, and sweetened iced teas, among others, leads to an increase in diabetes, heart disease, and cancers. Mexico had the highest rate of deaths that could be attributed to sugary drinks, with 405 deaths per 1 million adults, while the United States came in second, with a death rate of 125 per 1 million adults.

There are numerous types of sugar, and not all of them are bad for you.

Aspartame, the most popular artificial sweetener, was discovered accidentally in the 1960s by a researcher who was working on a treatment for stomach cancer.

Food makers use artificial sweeteners in baked goods, powdered drink mixes, puddings, jams, jellies, and processed foods. Most are sweeter than sugar, but without the calories. A person only has to use a tiny bit of artificial sugar to get the same level of sweetness as a teaspoon of real sugar. Many scientific studies

EDUCATIONAL VIDEO

NATURAL VERSUS ADDED SUGAR

Scan this code for a video about the difference between the natural and added sugar.

An agave plantation in Mexico. Agave is used to make sweetener, and also the alcoholic drink tequila.

suggest synthetic sweeteners are healthier than processed sugar, which is why there is a large global artificial sweetener market. Today it is currently around $1.5 billion.

Still, people wishing for a more natural alternative to sugar do not have to look far. Honey and maple syrup are two of the most popular natural sweeteners. However, there are others, including agave, a sweet sap of the agave plant; barley malt syrup, produced by cooking barley down until it becomes a thick liquid; and stevia, a shrub that is 30 times sweeter than processed sugar.

High fructose corn syrup (HFCS) is another sweetener that has become a flavorful alternative to sucrose. HFCS is made from corn and is chemically similar to sucrose. It does not break down in acidic foods and beverages, and it is less expensive than sucrose. Most people consume HFCS by drinking soda and other sweetened beverages. According to the Illinois Farm Bureau, the average American in 2009 consumed 35.7 pounds of high fructose corn syrup. Because it is a liquid, HFCS is extremely easy for manufacturers to use. It can be found not only in sodas, but also in applesauce, barbecue sauce, ketchup, and many other foods.

TEXT-DEPENDENT QUESTIONS

1. How many calories are in a teaspoon of processed sugar?
2. What is lactose?
3. Name two types of natural alternatives to sugar.

RESEARCH PROJECT

Keep track of the amount of sugar you consume in packaged food, candy, and sugary beverages, including soda, sports drinks, sweetened teas, and juices, for seven days. You can do this by reading the nutritional labels on each item. Write down the amount for each day. When the week has concluded, use the information you gathered and put it into a chart. What did you learn? What can you conclude?

CHAPTER 2

HISTORY, MANUFACTURE, AND USE

WORDS TO UNDERSTAND

abolitionist: an opponent of slavery.

antibiotics: bacteria-killing drugs.

culinary: relating to cooking and food.

domesticated: tamed.

osmosis: movement of a liquid through a membrane.

synthesis: the formation of chemical compounds through one or more chemical reactions.

About 10,000 years ago on the island of New Guinea, humans domesticated sugarcane for the first time. Previously, ancient humans could only enjoy the sweetness of sugar in the fruits that they picked from trees and bushes. But the people of New Guinea eventually figured out how to plant and cultivate fields of sugarcane. They picked the stalk of the plant and chewed its fiber.

The New Guineans used sugarcane not just as a source of culinary delight, but also as an elixir that they believed could cure any ailment and change people's moods. The New Guineans revered sugarcane so much that they created myths around it, including one that told the story of how the human race came to be. Priests even gulped sugar water from coconut shells during religious rituals.

A worker sharpens his machete at a sugar plantation in Puerto Rico, circa 1930s.

ISLAND HOPPING

As people moved from place to place, they brought sugarcane with them. The plant grew well in warm, moist climates drenched by rains. People in the mainland of Asia were growing sugarcane by around 1000 BCE. Fifteen hundred years later, people in India found a way to process sugarcane into a powder that they used as a medicine. As years passed, sugarcane continued its journey around the world. When an army conquered a region, for example, soldiers brought their knowledge of sugarcane cultivation and production with them. Muslim caliphs, or kings, were so taken with marzipan (a type of sweet paste made from crushed almonds and sugar) that one ruler built an entire mosque from it to showcase his wealth.

To say people in the Middle East loved sugar would be an understatement. They perfected the refining process, the basics of which we still use today. Workers toiled in unbearably hot weather to cut fields of sugarcane with scythes. Most were slaves captured during battle. When European crusaders went to the Middle East to oust Muslims from the Holy Land, they brought back many things, including sugar.

In Europe, only wealthy people consumed sugar. Europeans became addicted to what they called "white gold." But with the rise of the Ottoman Empire in the 1400s, and the animosity that existed between Muslims and Christians at the time, Europe's source of sugar dried up. The Europeans decided to set sail into the unknown, in part, to look for new sources of sugar. When Christopher Columbus arrived in Hispaniola on his second trip to the New World in 1493, he brought sugarcane with him, which he then planted. Those first plants would change world history.

It didn't take long for sugarcane to take root across the Western Hemisphere. People grew sugarcane in the Caribbean, South America, and North America. The climate of Brazil, for example, was well suited for the cultivation of the crop. But sugar production is labor-intensive, meaning that it needs a lot of human effort to accomplish. To meet the demand back home, the Europeans created a plantation system that relied on slave labor.

The hard labor of harvesting sugarcane was done by slaves for hundreds of years.

FROM PLANTATION TO SUGAR BOWL

The Europeans, particularly the Spanish and Portuguese, first enslaved thousands of Native Americans to work on the sugar plantations. Brazil, which at the time was a Portuguese colony, became the center of the sugar trade, making Portugal the world's largest sugar supplier to Europe. By 1612, Brazil was producing more than 19.8 million pounds of sugar a year. It was a brutal business. Slaves worked long hours in the hot sun. Many died, while others escaped.

When the total number of native slaves dwindled, the Europeans replaced them with slaves from West Africa. Beginning in 1505 and ending some 300 years later, slave ships docked in the New World with the new, cheap source of labor.

Sugar was an important part of the "Triangular Trade" that linked Europe, Africa, and the Americas. In the Americas, sugar was harvested and milled, and traders sent it to Europe aboard ships. Once unloaded, these ships were repacked with finished products and taken to Africa, where the goods were traded for more slaves. African slaves—at least those who survived the hellish sea crossing, known as the "Middle Passage"—were then brought to the Americas to work on the sugar plantations. Experts estimate that more than 11 million Africans were brought to the New World from the beginning of the slave trade until 1807. Of that number, more than half were forced to work on sugar plantations.

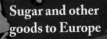

The Triangle Trade.

THE REAL PRICE OF SUGAR

Europeans were not blind to the brutal nature of sugar manufacturing. Voltaire, a French philosopher who lived in the 1700s, described the horrors of the sugar plantation in his novel *Candide*. In one passage, a slave describes working on the plantations. "When we work in the sugar mills and we catch our finger in the millstone, they cut off our hand; when we try to run away, they cut off a leg; both things have happened to me. It is at this price that you eat sugar in Europe."

In 1791 the British abolitionist William Fox called for a boycott of sugar grown by slaves in the British West Indies. "In every pound of sugar use, we may be considered as consuming two ounces of human flesh," he wrote. Fox's words inspired hundreds of thousands of Britons to stop using sugar, especially sugar produced in the Caribbean. Grocery store owners stopped selling sugar from the region. Instead, they imported sugar from India. Those who carried it home did so in containers emblazoned with the words "not made by slave labor."

Sugar barons colonized nearly every island in the Caribbean, including Puerto Rico, Trinidad, and Barbados. This region became the epicenter of the European sugar trade. Slaves planted sugarcane by digging trenches or holes and inserting sugarcane cuttings that were two-feet long. A gang of 30 slaves could plant two acres in a day. Then, at harvest time, the slaves cut the stalks, working night and day without any rest.

Sugar production, like any other commodity, was pushed along by a cycle of supply and demand. The more sugarcane the slaves planted and produced, the less expensive sugar became. This opened up new markets. Sugar was no longer the nobility's white gold—the lower classes were now able to afford sugar, too. But as consumption increased, so did the number of sugar plantations and slaves. Millions of people died in the sugarcane fields. Others died in the press houses as they extracted sugar juice from the cane. Many more died trying to escape bondage.

Despite these horrors, the sugar kept coming. On average, each Englishman consumed about 4 pounds of sugar a year in the early 1700s. A hundred years later that number had increased to 47 pounds.

A Tasty Grass

Processing sugar is a time-consuming job, although automation has made manufacturing much easier. Sugar is processed from two sources: sugarcane and sugar beets. Sugarcane is a tall grass that thrives in warm climates. Its stalks, which can grow upwards of 20 feet tall, brim with sucrose. The sugary liquid hides in the stem between the nodes from which the leaves emerge. In some climates, sugarcane reaches maturity in six months. In other environments, such as Louisiana, it takes two years. Eighty percent of the sugar we consume comes from sugarcane.

Once the stalks are ready for harvest, workers cut them, leaving the roots undamaged. The roots will sprout another generation the following year. Once harvested, field hands transport the cut cane to be processed.

The first step is to remove sucrose from the cane. To do this, workers put the stalks between large rollers called shredders, which crush and rip the cane apart. As the cane passes through the shredders, the sugar juice (sucrose) is squeezed out. Warm water is pumped through the system in the opposite direction to extract as much sugar juice

EDUCATIONAL VIDEO

HOW IS IT MADE?

Scan this code for a video about sugar production.

as possible. Next, the cane has to be milled, or crushed. Milling has to take place at least 24 hours after workers harvest the cane; otherwise the sucrose will start to dry.

Dirt and bits of cane contaminate the sugar juice, which means the sucrose has to be purified. Machines pump the sucrose through separators, which scrub the

Cane cutters in Jamaica, circa 1880s.

liquid clean. Afterward, workers send the juice to evaporators, large furnaces fueled by dried sugarcane fibers created during the shredding process.

As the juice heats up, its water boils off, creating a thick syrup. As the syrup evaporates, the sugar remains. Once the saturation point—the stage at which no more sugar can be dissolved in water—is reached, the crystallization process begins. Workers add a few granules of crystallized sugar to jumpstart that process. They call these grains *seed*.

Workers put the seed and the syrup in a centrifuge, which spins wildly, removing any liquid that might remain. As the syrup spins, it starts to crystallize into brown granules. These granules are taken to granulator, where they are purified and colored white. At this point, the crystals are large. They are then run through a series of screens, which makes them smaller and removes any impurities that might remain. The final result is pure cane sugar.

Variations in the refining process result in different types of sugar. For example, a type of sugar called turbinado is sugar that has been only partially refined. You might know turbinado sugar as the brown "raw sugar" packets that are found on some restaurant tables. But turbinado sugar is not actually brown sugar as cooks know it. True brown sugar, such as the type used in baking, contains molasses. White, granulated sugar, such as what you find on the dinner table, is created during the last step in the manufacturing process. Here are some other forms of refined sugar:

- **Confectioners' sugar.** Also known as powdered sugar, confectioners' sugar is granulated sugar ground to a fine powdered. The confectioners' sugar a baker uses to make cake icings and other treats is the finest of all the powdered sugars.
- **Coarse sugar.** Coarse sugar is recovered when sugar syrups, such as those containing high concentrations of molasses, are allowed to form into large crystals.
- **Sanding sugar.** Bakers use this type of sugar on top of their baked goods. The crystals are so large that they sparkle when struck by light.
- **Brown sugar.** This type of sugar has a high concentration of molasses syrup.

A sugar refinery in operation.

SUGAR BEET PROCESSING

Sugar beets are large tubular plants that contain a high concentration of sucrose in their roots. The process of turning sugar beets into processed sugar begins in the autumn and early winter, when farmers harvest the plants. Once they dig up the beets, workers slice the plant into thin pieces called *cossettes*. They then put the the cossettes into a special machine called a diffuser. Inside the diffuser, rushing water slams into the cossettes, churning them up and creating a sugary, pulp-like solution called *raw juice*.

Workers then pump the raw juice into large evaporators, Inside the evaporators, the raw juice is heated until it boils. The extra moisture in the raw juice evaporates, creating a thick syrup. Once the syrup is filtered for any impurities, it is once again boiled, creating a mixture of crystals and syrup called *massecuite*. Workers send the massecuite to centrifuges, where syrup is turned into crystals. They then use clean hot water to turn the crystals white, producing pure white sugar. After the sugar dries and all its moisture has dissipated, machines package the sugar and then trucks transport it to stores.

Uses for Sugar

Sugar enhances the sweetness of food. It is sweet because it contains various configurations of oxygen and hydrogen atoms that stimulate the sweetness taste receptors on our tongues.

Yet sugar can do a whole host of things besides providing food with a sweet taste. Sugar has the ability to stop microorganisms from forming, which is why it is used as a preservative in jams and jellies. Sugar causes bacteria to lose water through the process of osmosis. Without moisture, bacteria cannot grow and divide.

Sugar osmosis is the reason why people in the past used sugar to heal infected wounds. Even today, some doctors use sugar in their practice. In fact, Alan Bayliss, who

A street market in Machachi, Ecuador; the man on the left is selling blocks of raw sugar.

THE FIRST ARTIFICIAL SWEETENER

Saccharine was the first artificially made sweetener. As often happens, it was discovered completely by accident. One night in June 1878, a chemist named Constantin Fahlberg sat down to eat dinner. As he bit into a roll, he was struck by how sweet the crust tasted. Fahlberg was well qualified to measure the sweetness of food—he studied sugar at the H.W. Perot Import Co., in Baltimore, and worked alongside Ira Remsen, a professor of chemistry, at Johns Hopkins University.

As Fahlberg sat at the dinner table, he wondered why the roll was so sweet. Then it occurred to him: earlier in the day, he had spilled an experimental compound on his hands while working in Remsen's laboratory. Whatever he had on his hands had made its way to the dinner roll. Fahlberg rushed back to the laboratory and licked everything on his workbench. Finally, he found the source of the sweetness: a beaker of *o-sulfobenzoic acid* that had reacted with two other chemicals, *phosphorus chloride* and *ammonia*. The chemical reaction formed a third compound, *benzoic sulfinide*, better known as saccharine.

Fahlberg recreated the chemical reaction, and he and Remsen published a paper describing the synthesis. The scientists noted that the compound was "even sweeter than cane sugar."

Can an artificial sweetener also be natural? The makers of Splenda believe so, because, as its slogan claims, it's "Made from sugar, so it tastes like sugar." But Splenda, also known as sucralose, was first made in a laboratory. Sucralose is a thousand times sweeter than sucrose, and three times sweeter than saccharine. Although sucralose is synthesized from sugar, its molecular makeup is significantly different. Because of its chemical structure, the body does not digest sucralose. Consequently, sucralose has no nutritional value.

lives in Birmingham, England, owes his life to processed sugar. Doctors amputated Bayliss's right leg above the knee after he developed a large wound. However, the wound was not healing with standard antibiotics. Health-care workers at Moseley Hall Hospital applied sugar to the wound. The sugar sucked up the moisture in the wound, which stopped the spread of bacteria. The leg eventually healed.

Sugar also slows the freezing process by preventing large ice crystals from forming. Chefs put sugar in custards, puddings, and sauces not only for its sweet taste, but also to help break down proteins in egg whites so they can spread more evenly throughout the batter or saucy mixtures. As a result, the egg whites take their time to thicken, which is why puddings and custards are so smooth. Sugar also prevents starches in flour from forming into lumps. In addition, sugar is mixed in salad dressing to cut down on the acidity of vinegar or lemon juice that might be used in the recipe.

In 2014, engineers working in London's subway system used sugar to help clean off a layer of concrete that workers accidentally poured on some electrical equipment. Why did they use sugar? Sugar slows down the chemical reaction that causes concrete to set. For this reason, is often added to concrete mixtures when builders need to slow down the hardening process.

TEXT-DEPENDENT QUESTIONS

1. Where was sugarcane first domesticated?
2. What was the first artificial sweetener?
3. What are three uses for sugar, besides making food taste sweet?

RESEARCH PROJECT

Go onto the Internet and print out a black line map of the world. Then go online and research the top sugar producers on the planet. Shade in those areas where sugar is produced. What can you conclude?

CHAPTER
3

MEDICAL CONCERNS

WORDS TO UNDERSTAND

endocrinologist: doctor who specializes in treating disorders of the endocrine system, which produces hormones that keep the body running as it should.

energy sufficiency: the ratio between energy output and consumption

hormones: chemical messengers in the body.

metabolism: the chemical process by which living cells produce energy.

Every meal a person eats is a chance to fuel up. Food provides the body with the necessary energy it needs to run. As you read in chapter one, sugar is essential to life. In fact, health experts push people to eat more fruits and vegetables, all good sources of natural sugar, which the body turns into energy.

If that's the case, why do doctors and other health professionals have a problem with sugar? Why does study after study suggest that too much sugar is bad for your health? Why is natural sugar contained in a peach better for you than processed sugar contained in a candy bar?

For one thing, natural sugar in whole fruits and vegetables is not as highly concentrated as processed sugar. The sugars in fruits and vegetables are diluted by water, plant fiber, and other substances. Processed, or refined, sugar is stripped of all those elements along with its vitamins and minerals. That's why sugary

Refined sugar is called "empty calories" because it contains nothing that your body can actually use.

SUGAR IN THE WOMB

Sugar is sweet-tasting, even to fetuses in the womb. Inside the mother's womb, amniotic fluid surrounds the fetus. It acts as an air bag, cushioning the child. The fluid also helps the fetus develop its lungs, muscles, and digestive system. Sometimes there is too much amniotic fluid. It is a condition known as *polyhydramnios*. It can cause premature birth, stillbirth, and other problems. Doctors often treat polyhydramnios by injecting a sugary substance into the amniotic fluid. The fetus finds the solution sweet and pleasant. Consequently, it ingests more fluid, which it then passes out through the umbilical cord and the mother's kidneys, reducing the amount of amniotic fluid in the womb.

foods are often called "empty calories"—they don't have the nutritional value that foods with natural sugar have. Each bite of a candy bar or each sip of a soft drink contains a heavy dose of purified sugar that can quickly throw a monkey wrench into the body's metabolism.

Metabolism is how the body processes sugar. The body burns sugar as energy, known as glucose. Glucose fuels every process in the body, allowing cells to function and grow normally. However, the body turns extra sugar into fat, which it then stores for later use. Fats are organic compounds that supply calories to the body. While some fats (unsaturated) are good, others (saturated) are not. Bad fat can lead to weight gain and contribute to a variety of health issues, including high blood pressure, heart disease, stroke, various cancers, and osteoarthritis.

Flooding the body with processed sugar can overwhelm a person's metabolism. As a result, the body stores excess glucose as fat. Excess sugar can also cause a variety of health problems.

LINKING SUGAR TO BAD HEALTH

Doctors have always known there is a correlation between sugar and health. In 1675, as Europeans were consuming massive amounts of the "white gold," a British physician named Thomas Willis noticed that the urine of his diabetic patients was "wonderfully sweet, as if it were imbued with honey or sugar." In 1925, Columbia University's Haven Emerson noted that death rates among diabetic patients between 1900 and 1920 increased as sugar consumption grew.

The problem is that most processed sugar is made up of equal amounts of glucose and fructose. The body's cells metabolize glucose, but the liver is responsible for processing fructose. When the liver breaks fructose down, it produces bad fat called triglycerides. While some of that fat can stay in the liver and damage it, most triglycerides enter the bloodstream. The results can be deadly.

SUGAR AND CHOLESTEROL

All of the body's cells contain cholesterol, a fatty, wax-like substance the spurs the body to create hormones and other substances that help a person digest food. The body makes all the cholesterol it needs, however, and many people actually make more than they need. So excess cholesterol can be a very serious health issue. High cholesterol is one health problem that excess sugar can make worse.

Not all cholesterols are created equal. Some, notably triglycerides, are considered to be "bad" because they can clog a person's arteries and restrict blood flow to the heart. Good cholesterol, known as high-density lipoprotein (HDL) removes bad cholesterol from the blood. Researchers have found that those who consume a lot of sugar have high levels of bad cholesterol and lower levels of good cholesterol. Those who consume the least amount of sugar have lower levels of bad cholesterol. If the good and bad cholesterol are not in balance, a person can suffer from heart disease.

Too much cholesterol can also form plaque in the walls of arteries. Plaque creates a barrier that blood cannot pass through, and too much plaque can make

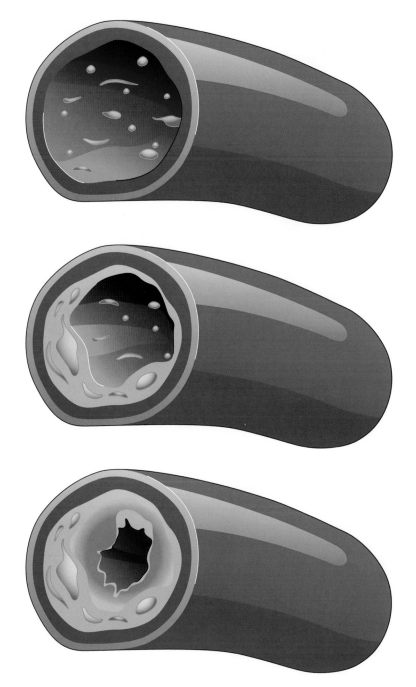

"Bad" cholesterol can block veins and arteries, leading to heart disease and other serious health problems.

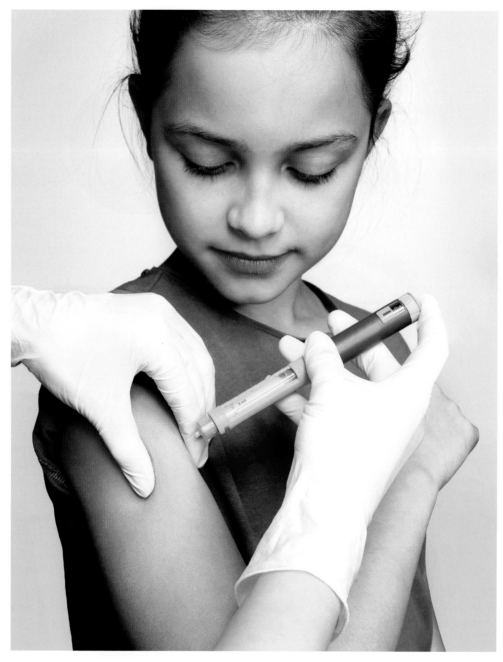

People with diabetes may need to inject the hormone called insulin because their bodies are not producing enough.

the heart work a lot harder than it has to as it pumps blood through the body. A bit of plaque can also break off and form a blood clot. A person can get a stroke if one of those clots walls off any artery moving blood to the brain. A stroke can result in partial paralysis, slurred speech, and death. A person can have a heart attack if a clot blocks an artery to the heart.

Diabetes, Hypoglycemia, and Hyperglycemia

Overloading the body with sugar can also interfere with its ability to regulate glucose levels in the blood (sometimes referred to as "blood sugar levels"). Glucose builds up in the bloodstream when a person eats foods containing a high concentration of sugar. The body, in an effort to balance itself out, responds by trying to get rid of the excess sugar. To do this, the body taps into its muscles to siphon off stored fat and proteins for energy, inhibiting the body's ability to convert glucose.

Diabetes can set in when the condition becomes severe. Diabetes occurs when the system that regulates blood sugar fails because of a lack of insulin. Insulin is a hormone produced in the pancreas that regulates the level of glucose in the blood. It also helps cells use glucose for energy. When there is too little insulin, glucose cannot travel to the cells. That disrupts the body's ability to burn glucose as energy. That's why diabetics must take insulin made in a laboratory. Although sugar itself does not cause diabetes, it can certainly make the problem worse.

EDUCATIONAL VIDEO

SUGAR AND HEALTH

Scan this code for a video about health concerns regarding sugar.

OPEN WIDE!

The shot of Novocain. The whirr of the dentist's drill. The pressure of metal on tooth. No one likes getting a cavity filled, but if you eat or drink a lot of sugar-laden food, chances are you have a cavity or two. Teeth begin to decay when bacteria inside the mouth feast on sugar. As bacteria multiply, tiny creatures produce an acid that damages the teeth.

The Diabetes Research Institute Foundation says 380 million people around the globe suffer from diabetes, including 29 million Americans. Scientists who have studied the relationship between dietary sugar and diabetes say that consuming just one sugary soda every day can increase a person's chances of developing diabetes by 1.1 percent.

Excess sugar also plays a role in conditions called hypoglycemia and hyperglycemia. When the pancreas is awash in sugar, it releases insulin to deal with it. The more sugar there is in the bloodstream, the more insulin the pancreas releases. When a person has too little blood sugar in their system, hypoglycemia develops. Hypoglycemia can lead to fatigue, forgetfulness, and poor concentration. Chances are you have experienced a brief bout of hypoglycemia in the past, such as feeling lightheaded before a meal. Once you ate, though, you felt better. That's because eating provided a rush of sugar that restored you body's natural glucose level. However, if hypoglycemia continues, it will harm organs and the body's systems, including the nervous and circulatory systems.

Consuming too much sugar can lead to hyperglycemia and increase the level of glucose in the bloodstream. When blood sugar is too high, a person might become unusually thirsty, urinate constantly, or have trouble seeing. Hyperglycemia can also damage the kidneys and heart.

OBESITY

Obesity, a condition in which excess body fat impacts a person's health, has become a major problem that affects one-third of the world's population, or roughly 2.1 billion people. Obesity is when a person's body mass index (BMI, a person's weight, in kilograms, divided by the square of his or her height, in meters) is greater than 30. Obesity is not the same as being overweight. An overweight person's BMI is between 25 and 29.9. Yet both are a serious concern for men, women, and children. In the United States, two-thirds of adults and one-third of children are either overweight or obese.

Obesity can lead to a number of health issues, including diabetes, high blood pressure, heart disease, arthritis, stroke, and gout, a joint disorder. Moreover, the more weight people carry around with them, the more stress they put on their

Researchers say that obesity has reached epidemic levels in the United States.

joints. Researchers have also found a correlation between obesity and some types of cancer. The American Heart Association found that obese children suffering from high cholesterol were more like to show early signs of heart disease. In a 2008 study, the artery walls of 70 obese children between the ages of 6 and 19 resembled those of a 45-year-old adult.

Dr. Robert Lustig, an **endocrinologist**, has an idea as to why this is. He blames sugar found in processed meals—and he is not alone in this theory. Lustig points out that over the years, people have increasingly come to rely on processed food. Accordingly, the consumption of sugar has skyrocketed, as have obesity rates.

As we have seen, when sugar overloads the body, insulin in the blood increases, forcing the body to store excess glucose in fat cells. This, Lustig says, slows down the production of leptin, a hormone produced in fat cells that essentially tells the brain to stop eating. If leptin is not available or is only available in dwindling amounts, the switch telling a person not to eat is never turned on.

FACTS ABOUT SODA

- During the 1970s, Americans received 4 percent of their daily caloric intake from sugary drinks. Thirty years later, that number had increased to 9 percent.
- While fruits and vegetables cost 35 percent more than 30 years ago (adjusted for inflation), soda costs 35 percent less.
- Each day, half of the nation's population drinks a sugary beverage.
- Another study found that every time a child drank a 12-ounce soda during the day, he or she increased the risk of becoming obese by 60 percent.
- Those who drink one or two cans of soda a day are 26 percent more likely to develop type 2 diabetes.

"When your leptin signal works, you're in energy balance, burning energy at a normal rate and feeling good," Lustig writes. "Every human has a 'personal leptin threshold,' above which the brain interprets a state of energy sufficiency." Consequently, when a person has the right amount of leptin in his or her system, that person has "appropriate appetite, normal physical activity, and feelings of well-being."

Sugary drinks are one big part of the sugar overload problem. According to researchers at Harvard University, the United States spends $190 billion a year to treat obesity-related diseases and conditions. Sugar-laden beverages, they say, are partly to blame. The beverages are sold in restaurants, grocery stores, convenience stores, and in schools. And over the decades, portions of sugary drinks have gotten bigger.

ARTIFICIAL SWEETENERS AND HEALTH

If sugar is a "poison," can a person win the battle of the bulge by using synthetic sugar substitutes? The answer is an unqualified "maybe."

Like sugar, artificial sweeteners are used in many processed foods and drinks. Unlike sugar, artificial sweeteners, such as saccharin, have virtually no calories and produce zero fat. For a time, people hoped that artificial sweeteners would be a "magic bullet" to cure all sugar-related health problems. Unfortunately, that has not turned out to be the case. Years of scientific studies have shed little light on whether artificial sweeteners are more healthful than natural ones.

In fact, people have been concerned for decades that artificial sweeteners could have a negative effect on health. In 2008 a U.S. government-funded study concluded that those who used artificial sweeteners gained more weight over a seven-to-eight-year period then those who did not consume sugar substitutes, mainly because people tended to consume more foods with sugar substitutes, thinking they were healthier.

The debate continues as to whether sugar substitutes are healthier than sugar.

Four years later, a study published in the *American Journal of Clinical Nutrition* concluded that those who used synthetic sweeteners had more problems with their metabolism than those who did not use them. Moreover, a 2013 study showed a causal link between artificially sweetened beverages and type 2 diabetes.

More recently, a 2014 study published in the journal *Nature* gave one reason why there was a link between artificial sweeteners and obesity. Researchers found that saccharine, one of the most widely used artificial sweeteners, can alter the composition of bacteria in the digestive system, forcing the body's glucose levels to rise and putting people at risk for diabetes.

But other studies have found that artificial sweeteners are harmless and safe to consume in limited qualities. The National Cancer Institute and other health agencies stress there is no scientific evidence to support the idea that artificial sweeteners are bad for a person's health. In the United States, the Food and Drug Administration (FDA) regulates artificial, or high-intensity, sweeteners. "Based on the available scientific evidence, the agency has concluded that the high-intensity sweeteners approved by FDA are safe for the general population under certain conditions of use," the FDA says on its website.

TEXT-DEPENDENT QUESTIONS

1. How does sugar impact diabetes?
2. What is the difference between hypoglycemia and hyperglycemia?
3. What is the importance of leptin?

RESEARCH PROJECT

Develop a list of your favorite sugary foods and find out the sugar content (the SELF NutritionData website, http://nutritiondata. self.com, can help). To visualize how much sugar is contained in each, you will need several packets of refined sugar (like those you get in a restaurant) or a box of sugar cubes. Depending on the brand, there will be between two and four grams of sugar in each packet or cube. Count the grams of sugar in each food. Then pile the correspondent packages of sugar up to visual how much sugar is in your favorite foods.

CHAPTER 4

CONSUMING SUGAR

WORDS TO UNDERSTAND

evolution: the process through which all species developed.

neurotransmitter: chemicals that carry messages between nerve cells.

toxic: poisonous.

There is no getting around it: too much sugar can be toxic. The evidence is overwhelming. Yet we humans adore, even crave, sugar. Why is that? Why do we continue to consume so much sugar even though it is bad for us? For many experts, the answer is simple: sugar, like heroin and cocaine, is addictive. In fact, sugar stimulates the same parts of the brain that respond to both of these drugs.

Let's be clear. All foods affect our brains—that's why we find certain foods tasty and others not so much. But sugary foods are different. Sugar turns up the volume, so to speak, to the point where our brains and bodies desire more sugar. How did we get to such a place? The answer lies millions of years in our past, when our ancient ancestors needed fructose to survive.

At the time, food was in short supply. Our ancient ancestors survived on fructose contained in fruits they picked from trees and bushes. At the time, sugar was a rare source of energy, but humans still craved it. Because of these cravings, humans looked for sweet things to eat. Over time, evolution found a way to turn sugar in the

About three-quarters of the packaged foods on supermarket shelves contain some added sugar.

bloodstream to fat. That was okay back then, because humans needed plenty of fat to survive when food was scarce.

When sugar became easier to find and produce, it hit our species like a sweet-tasting tsunami. Today, an estimated 75 percent of processed food contains sugar. On average, each American consumes a quarter to a half pound of sugar a day.

Our brains now hardwired to enjoy the pleasing, almost euphoric effect of sugar. Here's why: the minute a person bites into a piece of candy or drinks a cola, sugar sends a signal to the brain. The message moves quickly over a series of electrical and chemical transmission lines until the brain's pleasure centers are stimulated. Sugar makes you feel good, just like a drug. It affects the brain by enhancing the effects of a **neurotransmitter** called dopamine. Neurotransmitters are chemicals that allow billions of nerve cells, or neurons, to communicate with each other. Dopamine is sometimes called a "feel good" neurotransmitter, because it is connected to our ability to experience pleasure. Every time you eat a tasty meal, your body releases dopamine into the brain. Interestingly, if you ate the same meal day after day, the amount of dopamine would level off. That once-yummy meal won't be as tasty any longer, because you would not be getting as much dopamine.

Sugar overstimulates the neurons, just like cocaine and heroin. The result is that an individual craves more sugar to satisfy their craving. They become addicted, although the effect is not nearly as pronounced as it is for a drug addict. Yet mice addicted to sugar not only crave it, but also binge on it. When it is taken away, they have withdrawal symptoms—a sign of physical dependence.

ECONOMICS OF SUGAR DEPENDENCE

The American Heart Association recommends that added sugar in processed food make up no more than half of the extra calories a person consumes each day from snacks. That equals out to 100 calories, or

Some medicines have sugar added.

U.S. SUGARY DRINK CONSUMPTION

In the United States, the consumption of sugary drinks has skyrocketed within the last 40 years. A significant part of this increase is due to the size of the drinks we buy. Between 1977 and 1996, for example, drink portions increased from 13.6 fluid ounces to 21.0 fluid ounces. Not only did the size increase, but so did the number of servings. In 1977, Americans drank 1.96 servings of sugar drinks each day. By 1996, that number had increased to 2.39 servings. From 1998 to 1996, the average American consumed 158 calories every day from sugar drinks. Within a decade, that number had jumped to 203 calories.

6 teaspoons, for women, and 150 calories, or 10 teaspoons, for men. Yet cutting down on added sugar is easier said than done.

Even health-conscious people who watch what they eat may not realize how much sugar they consume in a given day. Nonfat food is laden with sugar to enhance taste. Drug makers even coat pills with sugar and pour sugary solutions into children medications. Because of added sugar, countries are finding that the cost of health care has skyrocketed. According to a 2015 Morgan Stanley Research report, Europe spends 24 percent of its health-care costs treating diabetes-related maladies. North and Central America spend 51 percent, while South America spends only 5 percent. "Diabetes, obesity and their complications result in long-term care costs, often including hospitalization, a doubling down on high-cost medical care and lost work hours. Governments, employers and patients end up sharing the burden," the report states.

Moreover, diabetes and obesity can drag down a nation's economy because of increased health-care costs and a decrease in worker productivity. The Morgan Stanley report states that if sugar consumption does not decrease in countries like

Chile, Mexico, the United States, Australia, New Zealand, and others, they all will lose a significant percentage of their gross domestic product (GDP), a measure of all the goods and services a country produces. Researchers have predicted that by 2035, Chile's GDP will decline by 33 percent, while the United States will lose about 24 percent of its economic output.

Another strategy for keeping sugary drinks away from kids is to keep these drinks out of school vending machines.

EDUCATIONAL VIDEO

SUGAR SECRETS

Scan this code for more health facts about sugar.

A TAXING SITUATION

In recent years, governments have sought to decrease the use of certain unhealthful products, such as tobacco and alcohol, by adding taxes to make them more expensive to purchase. The idea is that if a product is too expensive, people will use less of it.

When it comes to tobacco products, such "sin taxes" have worked. In the United States, a 10 percent increase in cigarette taxes has cut the number of lung cancer deaths by 1.5 percent, according to the World Health Association. In France, an increase in cigarette taxes corresponded with a 50 percent reduction in lung cancer deaths for males.

Because of the success of tobacco taxes, states and cities have resorted to taxing sugary food and beverages in the hope that people will buy less of them. According to the Council of State Governments, 34 states and the District of Columbia tax sodas sold in stores, while nearly 40 states tax soda sold in vending machines. Arkansas, Missouri, Utah, and Virginia tax soft drinks at a much higher rate than the general sales tax rate. Some states tax soda distributors, while still others tax wholesalers, retailers, and manufacturers.

Still, according to the Public Health Law Center at William Mitchell College of Law, regardless of the type of tax, soda taxes "have no meaningful impact on the consumption of sugar drinks and related weight outcomes." The center says that the taxes are too low to decrease consumption in any meaningful way.

While taxing soda is one approach, many communities are trying other programs. In 2016, for example, San Francisco began to require warning labels on advertisements for sugar-sweetened drinks.

BIG SUGAR

Trying to get people off sugar is at times an uphill battle. Sugar tastes good, but according to the Union of Concerned Scientists (UCS), it is not the only reason why Americans consume so much of it. In their view, the sugar industry, which includes manufacturing groups, marketing executives, trade associations, and government lobbying groups, among others, desperately want to keep Americans addicted to their product. According to the UCS, the industry tries to keep Americans in the dark about how much sugar they are consuming or what the effect of that consumption might be.

The UCS says the sugar industry not only disregards science, but also allegedly lies as it tries to undermine public anti-sugar policies. It also says the industry has been a bulwark against adapting nutritional standards and food policies to address the scientific evidence on the health risks of added sugar.

"To challenge and overcome sugar interests' efforts to undermine the science and policy around sugar's adverse health impacts, several actors can play a role in ensuring that science-based health and nutrition policies are enacted," the UCS said in its 2014 report titled *Added Sugar, Subtracted Science*.

Specifically, the scientists are asking the U.S. Surgeon General to compile a report on added sugar and its impact on health. Among other things, the scientists also called on the federal government, states, and local communities to conduct a public awareness campaign to counter the "misinformation from [the] sugar interests" and provide the public with sound scientific information.

Sodas are not the only problem. For example, kids' cereals can be as much as 50 percent pure sugar.

NOT SO SWEET IN PHILLY

Interestingly, when Philadelphia became the first major city in the United States to tax soda and other sugary beverages, lawmakers did not focus on the health benefits of reducing sugar consumption. Instead, they framed the debate in economic terms, arguing the city would see an increase in revenue from the new tax, which is expected to raise $91 million a year.

"What we're looking to do is to take some of that profit, to put it back into the neighborhoods that have been their biggest customers, to improve the lives and opportunities for the people who live there," Mayor Jim Kenney said at a rally in support of the measure.

In response, the American Beverage Association said it would "take legal action to stop it." In its view, the tax "unfairly singles out beverages, including low- and no-calorie choices. The fact remains that these taxes are discriminatory and highly unpopular — not only with Philadelphians, but with all Americans."

SWEET CHEMICALS

The next time you are in the supermarket, look at the nutritional label on a pack of sugar-free gum. You might be amazed at what you find in its list of ingredients. Many sugar-free foods contain more than one artificial sweetener. One brand of sugar-free gum, for example, includes aspartame, acesulfame K, and sucralose. Why so many? Artificial sweeteners boost the sweetness of one another, which is why food makers include more than one sweetener in many products.

Sugar-free gum is sweetened artificially.

Many Philadelphians were incensed at the idea of a soda tax. As in many other places, including New York City, many people felt the tax was an example of government overreach. In their view, drinking a sugary beverage, no matter the size, was a personal choice that the government had no right to infringe upon.

Still, the tax could go a long way in making the city a healthier place. "Obesity and poverty are both intractable national problems," former New York City mayor Michael Bloomberg said when the council passed the bill. Bloomberg spent $1.6 million in support of Mayor Kenney's initiative. "No policy takes more direct aim at both than Philadelphia's tax on sugary drinks."

TEXT-DEPENDENT QUESTIONS

1. How does sugar affect the brain?
2. Name some of the public policy initiatives that communities have taken to reduce the amount of sugar in people's diets.
3. Explain why sugar consumption has the potential to drag down the economy.

RESEARCH PROJECT

Research and give an oral report either in support or in opposition to the implementation of taxes on sugary beverages. Make sure that your arguments are logical, convincing, and clear. Cite facts that support your position.

FURTHER READING

Books and Articles

Abbott, Elizabeth. *Sugar: A Bittersweet History*. New York: Overlook Press, 2011.

Aronson, Marc, and Marina Budhos. *Sugar Changed the World: A Story of Magic, Spice, Slavery, Freedom, and Science*. New York: Clarion Books, 2010.

California Department of Public Health. *The CDC Guide to Strategies for Reducing the Consumption of Sugar-Sweetened Beverages*. http://www.cdph.ca.gov/SiteCollectionDocuments/StratstoReduce_Sugar_Sweetened_Bevs.pdf.

Mayo Clinic Staff. "Artificial Sweeteners and Other Sugar Substitutes." August 20, 2015. http://www.mayoclinic.org/healthy-lifestyle/nutrition-and-healthy-eating/in-depth/artificial-sweeteners/art-20046936.

O'Connell, Jeff. *Sugar Nation: The Hidden Truth behind America's Deadliest Habit and the Simple Way to Beat It*. New York: Hyperion, 2011.

Peña, Carolyn de la. *Empty Pleasures: The Story of Artificial Sweeteners from Saccharine to Splenda*. Chapel Hill: University of North Carolina Press, 2011.

The Sugar Association. "Refining and Processing Sugar: Consumer Fact Sheet." https://www.sugar.org/images/docs/refining-and-processing-sugar.pdf.

Woman and Childrens' Health Network. "Sugar—Yes, You're Sweet Enough!" http://www.cyh.com/HealthTopics/HealthTopicDetailsKids.aspx?p=335&np=284&id=2685.

Websites

Discovery Kids. "Activity: Rock Candy. "
http://discoverykids.com/activities/rock-candy/
Another great science experiment; this one shows you how to make rock candy.

Science for Kids. "How Sweet It Is."

http://www.scienceforkidsclub.com/sugar-experiment.html

A cool science experiment that will illustrate how much sugar you eat each day.

SugarScience: The Unsweetened Truth

http://www.sugarscience.org/

Sponsored by the University of California, San Francisco, this site collects a large amount of useful data about the health impact of sugar.

EDUCATIONAL VIDEOS

Chapter One: Prevention. "Sugar Showdown: Whole vs. Processed Foods." https://youtu.be/Du1TDSJ2sy0.

Chapter Two. How It's Made. "Sugar." https://youtu.be/0QRmJQoI-xU.

Chapter Three: BBC Productions. "The Truth about Sugar." https://youtu.be/ONXNKacNU_4.

Chapter Four: CBC News. "The Secrets of Sugar." https://youtu.be/K3ksKkCOgTw.

SERIES GLOSSARY

amino acid: an organic molecule that is the building block of proteins.

antibody: a protein in the blood that fights off substances the body thinks are dangerous.

antioxidant: a substance that fights against free radicals, molecules in the body that can damage other cells.

biofortification: the process of improving the nutritional value of crops through breeding or genetic modification.

calories: units of energy.

caramelization: the process by which the natural sugars in foods brown when heated, creating a nutty flavor.

carbohydrates: starches, sugars, and fibers found in food; a main source of energy for the body.

carcinogen: something that causes cancer.

carnivorous: meat-eating.

cholesterol: a soft, waxy substance present in all parts of the body, including the skin, muscles, liver, and intestines.

collagen: a fibrous protein that makes up much of the body's connective tissues.

deficiency: a lack of something, such as a nutrient in one's diet.

derivative: a product that is made from another source; for example, malt comes from barley, making it a barley derivative.

diabetes: a disease in which the body's ability to produce the hormone insulin is impaired.

emulsifiers: chemicals that allow mixtures to blend.

enzyme: a protein that starts or accelerates an action or process within the body.

food additive: a product added to a food to improve flavor, appearance, nutritional value, or shelf life.

genetically modified organism (GMO): a plant or animal that has had its genetic material altered to create new characteristics.

growth hormone: a substance either naturally produced by the body or synthetically made that stimulates growth in animals or plants.

herbicide: a substance designed to kill unwanted plants, such as weeds.

ionizing radiation: a form of radiation that is used in agriculture; foods are exposed to X-rays or other sources of radiation to eliminate microorganisms and insects and make foods safer.

legume: a plant belonging to the pea family, with fruits or seeds that grow in pods.

macronutrients: nutrients required in large amounts for the health of living organisms, including proteins, fats, and carbohydrates.

malnutrition: a lack of nutrients in the diet, due to food inaccessibility, not consuming enough vitamins and minerals, and other factors.

marketing: the way companies advertise their products to consumers.

metabolism: the chemical process by which living cells produce energy.

micronutrients: nutrients required in very small amounts for the health of living organisms.

monoculture farming: the agricultural practice of growing a massive amount of a single crop, instead of smaller amounts of diverse crops.

nutritional profile: the nutritional makeup of given foods, including the balance of vitamins, minerals, proteins, fats, and other components.

obesity: a condition in which excess body fat has amassed to the point where it causes ill-health effects.

pasteurization: a process that kills microorganisms, making certain foods and drinks safer to consume.

pesticide: a substance designed to kill insects or other organisms that can cause damage to plants or animals.

processed food: food that has been refined before resale, often with additional fats, sugars, sodium, and other additives.

protein complementation: the dietary practice of combining different plant-based foods to get all of the essential amino acids.

refined: when referring to grains or flours, describing those that have been processed to remove elements of the whole grain.

savory: a spicy or salty quality in food.

subsidy: money given by the government to help industries and businesses stay competitive.

sustainable: a practice that can be successfully maintained over a long period of time.

vegan: a person who does not eat meat, poultry, fish, dairy, or other products sourced from animals.

vegetarian: a person who does not eat meat, poultry, or fish.

whole grain: grains that have been minimally processed and contain all three main parts of the grain—the bran, the germ, and the endosperm.

INDEX

ABOUT THE AUTHOR

John Perritano is an award-winning journalist, writer, and editor from Southbury, CT. He has written numerous articles and books on a variety of subjects including science, sports, history, and culture for such publishers as Mason Crest, National Geographic, Scholastic, and Time/Life. His articles have appeared on Discovery.com, Popular Mechanics.com, and other magazines and websites. He holds a Master's Degree in American History from Western Connecticut State University.

PHOTO CREDITS